Heaven and Earth

Poems
Written by Lisa-Renee

Heaven and Earth
© 2024
All rights reserved

Cover Image: Lisa-Renee
Cover Design: Lisa-Renee
Layout: IngramSpark

Printed in the U.S.A
First Edition: 9/16/2024
ISBN: 979-8-3303-4195-5

https://lrenterprises.net
www.ingramspark.com

For SJ

*Thank you for the advice and encouragement that
helped bring Heaven closer to Earth.*

Life Beats

Music is everywhere these days, at the touch of a button,
A tune for every feeling the heart conceives,
With a rhythm that seems to wake the deepest self;
We are drawn to music, seeking a Life Beat.

Where does this magic rhythm find us in the world,
And when does it first beat upon our souls like a drum?
Why have humans always sought this divine percussion,
To move our spirits like dancers in each moment?

From the time we are first held, in the center of another life,
There is the beat that we hear before a single note,
A warm and thriving beat of the first person to love us
Is the truest rhythm we will ever hear on earth.

If memories are like songs, the hazy melodies we hum,
Not always certain of every note or word,
The Life Beat is the pulse that runs through space,
Time, and the Eternal in perfect harmony.

The Bridge to Forever

As a child, I remember a place
Where my mind and heart were one,
A quiet wood surrounding an ancient lake,
Where I walked the bridge to forever.
I recall the colors of that place,
The rainbow of green hues in every tree
To signify so many phases of life,
The diamond shine of the water below
To give a calm reminder of eternity.

Through my life I have been walking,
And searching for this bridge again.
When dream and memory merge
Like the silent forest and endless water,
I remember the place, as a child.

Cathedral of the Saints

The dawn enters my room,
Waking all of my senses
Like the church bell that chimes
From a distant parish tower.

With careful pace, I rise and prepare
For a special morning of worship.
No homily or processional,
But a journey of spiritual communion.

Driving through town at sunrise,
I am a solitary pilgrim.
Passing steeples tall and proud,
My church still lies ahead.

Miles down the road I see it,
Emerging from the empty hills
And reflecting the sunshine
Like a pane of heavenly glass.

Reaching the place, I slow and stop,
Pausing for a moment to reflect,
Approaching then with a whispered
Kyrie Eleison.

I enter this holy site in silence,
Though I only imagine the doors
As I pass through and within.
Even my breath is joined by sacred echoes
Of others who have prayed here.

Before me lies a frozen space
Where countless souls, sleeping and awake,
Gather to remember names and places
Of heroes and their glorious victories.

I walk among them slowly,
Taking care to meet with smiles for the living,
Or a gentle hand for those at rest.
I glimpse heaven here – the joining of earth and sky.

For a moment my gaze turns up
To thank the Father who watches over
This field of stone and earth,
The Cathedral of the Saints.

Requiem

You are gone from me, and yet I see you everywhere,
Not as haunting vision nor vivid fancy of the mind,
But in the quiet world that surrounds me in this place
Where I retreat to give you sacred space and time.

You are resting in the silent ground beneath my feet,
In peaceful sleep as we did, wearing passion's warm glow.
You are moving in the trees as I watch them gently dance,
With silent grace the way you once danced with me.
You are looking down through the topaz sky,
As blue as your eyes that looked at me with love.
You are living now in my heart's most sacred place,
The same as when I heard your heart beating with mine.

What I Did Wrong

I didn't understand myself
                    When I became a part of his life
I didn't tell him my pain
                    When he asked me about my life
I didn't show him all of me
                    When he wondered what I want from life
I didn't share what I need
                    When he invited me to share his life
I didn't say how it hurt me
                    When he stopped trying in his life
I didn't have anything left
                    When he kept despairing over life

He never really knew me.
Then it was too late.
That's what I did wrong.

Ask, Try, Listen

Ask the questions, about everything you can.
Ask why the world is the way it is.
Ask until you run out of breath.

Try all the things your mind can fathom.
Try and take the risks that seem impossible.
Try until you can go no further.

Listen to every feeling that moves you.
Listen with both ears and heart.
Listen until you find the answers.

To Be Wise

Regarding life and what it brings us,
How often we gaze and wonder at it,
As a child does a brilliant new toy
And wonders how best to play with it.

So, too, is the discovery of wisdom.
In our youth, we take this new life
In selfish, hungry mouthfuls - not in greed,
But desperate fear that it does not last.

We are right to know this, but not to fear it,
For only God will place the limits of Life,
Love, and Death around each beating heart
To guide each course from earth to heaven.

If we have wisdom, then our hands are open,
When once we might have closed them tight
To keep life's precious jewel for ourselves,
And now, we see its fullest beauty.

To be wise is not to prevent the unknown,
Or make recompense for days gone by.
To live, to love, to know…this is wisdom.

Yin and Yang, Man and Woman

Many stories tell of eternity and creation,
That the Great Power seeks to give of Itself in abundance
To receive love from Its earthly life so fearfully made,
And so, the world begins with man and woman.
In this story, the first woman is the dark and silent water,
Passive yet deep and powerful to sustain life.
The first man is the light, strength and fire
That is made to move upon the water and give form to the land.
A new firmament takes its place as man and woman are joined
Above the earth as sky, sun, moon, and stars.
Man on earth is the struggle for survival and conquest,
Though he is missing an essential piece of himself,
he cannot name it.
Woman is the urge for ground, warmth and comfort,
And she also requires a part of something, of someone, unknown.
When brought together, man and woman are opposites,
Forces of dragon and tiger, sky warrior and jungle mother,
But each holding the piece that completes the other.
This Yin and Yang, this Man and Woman bound together,
Are the magic of a universe conceived in Love.

The Boy Remembers

A little boy enters a great big world,
Brilliant light and booming sounds,
So many things to captivate his mind
That he can hardly wait to explore.
He is already full of laughter and tears,
As if he somehow expects the future.

Time passes, and the boy find new use
For humor and for pain as his world changes.
As strength and talent emerge from his heart,
He must start giving of himself to the world.
Life and love become complicated things,
But he knows that he will find them both.

Soon the boy knows trials and tribulations,
Hurtful words and deeds to pierce him,
And the anguish of the world will inspire
Only strength, love, and courage in his heart.
Not everyone will understand, he thinks,
Yet he strives for a life he can be proud of.

Many years and stories are now behind him,
Beautiful scenes and songs of joy and sorrow,
Though he is still missing something
Unknown as he travels the world to find it.
And suddenly, another soul still traveling
Gives life to the dream of love he remembers.

The Goddess

She is art, she is beauty, she lives in
The eloquent spirit of the poet.
Her divinity takes two forms,
One of water and one of earth.
The sea is the Golden Dragon's lair,
Where she reigns as his queen.
Beauty and power calms him,
Her love tames the trembling sea.
Earth is the artful human's realm,
Finding her ethereal voice in song.
Storytellers write of her in tribute,
Her wisdom is a gift to the world.
The flow of life is her teaching,
Her practice is the dance of existence.

Keeper of the Flame

Unguided love is a capricious spark,
Love from Heaven a constant flame.

May I keep the flame of creation,
Helping breathe life into others
With the same fire inside my heart.

May I build the flame of devotion,
Never allowing fear of loss or pain
To shield my heart from true love.

May I accept the flame of sacrifice,
A purifying trial in earthly life
By which my soul is perfected.

May I pass the flame of redemption,
The warm glow of comfort and mercy
For the world to know eternal joy.

5:00 AM

Before dawn, as darkness falls
To the edges of rising daylight,
Quiet, cool pockets of night linger,
Sleeping like the puppy at my feet.
Get up, pour coffee, breathe, and imagine,
Magic and miracles wait here
In this time between moon and sun,
When all possibilities are before you.

If All We Have Are Words

If all we have are words,
Clever phrases and sentimental rhymes,
To tell our love story to the world outside,
I will write until I run out of words.

If all we have are smiles,
Gentle hugs or a hidden touch of hands
To convey our passion to each other,
I will seek you until my heart stops beating.

If all we have is love,
The word so often misused and insincere,
To know that we have found it true,
I will say it in my heart forever.

Art Is Love

Dialogue is Love…
Words of joy, elation, pain, or despair
Have power to break the proud soul,
And help the right souls bind together.

Music is Love…
Notes and lyrics, harmony and rhythm
Have power to stir the open heart,
And help the right hearts sing together.

Comedy is Love…
Timing and punchlines, funny face and voices,
Have power to awaken the mind,
And help the right minds laugh together.

Dance is Love…
Movement and passion, couples or a solo,
Have power to captivate the body,
And help the right bodies orbit together.

Art is Love.

Stronger Than Steel

On the outside, she's exactly what men expect,
Sugar and Spice, and everything nice,
But the heart of this lady is stronger than steel.

She's been brought up to fear being too real,
Of losing the man she wants because he's weak
And can't take a girl who's as strong as him.

For years she's played a convincing role for him,
Pretending to like everything her man does,
Convincing herself that this is how love works.

The early parts of their life seemed perfect,
When he felt loved and supported by his woman,
And she knew one day it would be her turn.

Life gets less than perfect, for both of them,
But when she needs the man to support her,
He blames her for not being what he needed.

Then, much later, in a new phase of her life,
She realizes her voice is louder than ever before,
And her heart will always be stronger than steel.

Afternoon Song

I had a dream about you.

It started at sunrise, and I was headed down a dirt road
In my old pickup with my guitar on the seat beside me.

Suddenly I pulled off the road and stopped,
Not quite knowing what I wanted to do
Or why I needed to stop and wait there,
But the sun was warm as I rested on the grass.

Was it minutes or hours I waited,
Thinking of nothing in particular?
Only the noise of a nearing motor
Broke my silent pause, as the sun reached noon.

And there you were, climbing out
Of a sturdy truck and scanning the fields.
Then you walked over in silence,
Taking a seat beside me.

I thought of picking wildflowers,
Counting clouds or braiding leaves of grass,
But I only breathed and listened.
You smiled and ran your fingers across the ground.

Then I turned to you and watched your face,
Every small movement of your eyes,
Each silent dance of your mouth as you smiled.
"I've missed you," it said.

We met at your front porch and sat down
To strum and sing familiar songs.
Soon we found the sun retreating
And put our songs to bed for the night.

Then we watched a crackling fire
While you read your favorite book aloud,
And I listened, with my heart, to the words
As I rested my head on your shoulder.

Falling asleep on the rocking chair,
I could feel a soft blanket surround me,
As the fire's embers were dying,
And I dreamed of our afternoon song.

Real Love, Real Life

"Wake up and join the real world," they told me,
And I thought I was awake, in a real world,
Work, friends, love, life, everything seemed real.
Except when it didn't, when something felt fake,
I saw others happy, but I wasn't, not really,
And I knew they wouldn't believe me, thinking
"You're so lucky, to really have everything!"
So I let them believe what they thought was real,
Even when I couldn't make it real for myself.
"Give up and accept the reality," I told myself,
As I lived for things where I could find an escape,
But why was I trying to escape my real life?
And later, when real love walked in the door,
I told myself that even this one real thing
Couldn't be real, because it would risk everything.
Now I know what is real, both life and love,
Because now I know the truth is worth everything.

Life and Death

At sunrise, I walk alone,
Out among listening trees and watching skies,
And soon approach in silence,
Darkness, a deep recess in quiet earth.
Look above me, there is life,
Light and sound of a waking world.
Gaze below, there is death,
The dusk and slumber unending.
Where do these elements meet?

Each breath, each step on the human path -
This is the matter of life and death.
A hole in the ground, a well or a grave,
Where either benefit or suffering is gained.
Life will draw its living from the well,
Satisfied by joy that can he shared.
Death will throw itself into the grave,
Forsaking all, no thirsting soul is spared.
The choice of life or death is mine.

Now That I Love You

Now that I met you
Like Aquarius and Pisces
Our own journeys so near
I wonder at the timing
Of this point in destiny.

Now that I know you
Like Amethyst and Garnet
Our mutual gifts so rare
I wonder at the sharing
Of these hearts and souls.

Now that I love you
Like Earth and Sun
Our own perfection grows
I wonder at the idea
Of ever being without you.

Coffee and Crème Brulee

I imagine Paris when you smile at me.
A single red rose, for La Vie en Rose,
Life and love we sang about,
Over Café Gourmand, slightly bitter,
Dancing in my mouth with Crème Brulee.
You are the flavor of laughter to me,
The burst of a punchline, breaking the shell,
Revealing a warm sweetness inside.
So many notes and layers of you,
Each one leaves me hungry for more.

The Writers

Two people, a man and a woman,
Made words the frame of their world.

He traveled many roads, she a straight line,
Neither was the path they always hoped to find.

The man gathered stories and memories,
Words of love in many forms, but incomplete.

The woman played many roles in life,
Words of art in many hues, but without light.

He longed to tell his story, both to the world
And to the one he prayed his soul would love.

She looked beyond her stage, to her own words,
And to the one she prayed would free her heart.

Soon, a miracle would transfigure their words,
Spoken thoughts, silent dreams, a hidden universe.

He found her, she found him, with sudden revelation,
Love so real, so bright, so pure and unashamed.

These writers, now with one love, soul and mind,
Will share the path they always hoped to find.

La Palma Sunset

Meeting you that day, under the yellow sun
That warmed my skin on crystal white sands,
Fresh plantains and mangos with light wine,
A refreshing splash of new possibility,
Left us with a taste for more decadent fare.

Shopping in the mercado, under an azure sky,
I thought of blue, your eyes, that stare,
The deep topaz water I wanted to surround me
After a brief kiss, and a promise for later,
With the exotic breeze tempting my appetite.

Waiting by the shore as the day began to fall,
Rose colored satin draped my shoulders
When you found me there and took my hand.
An Edge of Night Hibiscus you placed in my hair
To match the blush of unspoken desire.

Feeling a surge of flame with the first caress,
Like a tender marigold you held me there
And glowed in the tangerine candlelight,
Slow but trembling passion to be one
Pursued us into love's enticing shadow.

Watching this warm romance overtake us,
Every pink blushing part of me became a ruby,
A treasure of dark and delicious jewels for you.
You savored me like pomegranate on your lips,
My ardor bloomed, my body a crimson rose.

Surpassing all colors of fire and sky together,
Mystical amethyst in the shade of night all around
Us as our love's craving was satisfied,
Night drew its soft and purple veil over this moment
As I gently moved with you in the land of dreams.

Saturday Together

On a quiet day, on a quiet street,
I met you under a cool oak tree.
Blue like a summer sky,
The flash of your eyes to mine,
Gentle music in every moment
With hands so restless to touch.
A day of walking through the world,
We cared nothing for time or topic,
Only the song of our voices together
Over sips of coffee and sightseeing.
City sounds crashed like waves,
Never more than echoes like a seashell
As everything said, "I Love You."
Kisses at a corner table, holding hands,
Perfect words in loving whispers
Between a sweet and simple pair,
Always together, as timeless as the stars
Reflected in a golden candle's flame.

Heaven and Earth

Let us be Heaven and Earth.
Speak the desires of your soul,
Let us leave no shadow hidden,
We are Sun God and Moon Goddess.

Let us be Hero and Villain.
Love is the ultimate freedom,
You are Jekyll and Hyde,
I am Queen and Concubine.

Let us be Yin and Yang in harmony.
Command me and be my slave,
I will drink your dragon's fire,
You will feast in my tiger's lair.

Let us be Eden and Nirvana.
Share with me all blessings and curses,
You are the holy place I seek,
I am your garden of pleasure.

Let us be Alpha and Omega.
You are a blinding world of light,
I am a raging river of life,
Let us be Creator God and Mother Earth.

Sonnet

As silent as the dawn I come to you,
Your eyes undress me, even from afar.
I lose all strength when taken in your arms,
The dance of love between us has begun,
My lips are parted, open now to you,
A kiss entwines our breathing, now as one.
Our bodies move together as we touch,
With hands that write a love song on warm skin,
And now you are inside me, deep within,
You penetrate my body, mind, and soul.
We look into each other's eyes with love,
Now at the point of passion's sweet release.
At last, our flame of love succumbs to bliss.
Our hearts will feel no greater joy than this.

Love Is Ageless

Since time began, I have loved you, my darling;
In my heart, love is ageless, and so are you.
With a look from your eyes, time fades away,
Any moment becomes the one that we share.
You are both the end and the beginning of my life,
A farewell to solitude, a greeting to true love.

You Are Love

Come to me, love, as you desire,
Not of obligatory stone or by rote;
As the wind I hope to cool me
Do I ask you ask for you, love's river,
To carry me across the earth.

Walk across a field, my love,
But do not rush to meet me;
Blooming joy is all around you
Which waits for gathering arms,
So patiently collect love's gift.

You are Love, and Love is You;
Do not hurry - come to me in God's time,
Find your home, and stay.

Blue

From the hazy blue horizon
I watched you fix your gaze,
Hold the perfect sky,
And show me an open world.

Touchstone

My perfect standard of love
All comparison ends with you
Affection's softest touch
The truest serenade
I long for your endless joy
Ceasing my wandering path
Returning to your heart
The world can turn away
My eyes no longer seek it
You exist and become the world

My Lover Shares My Soul

My lover shares my soul with me.
He is the journey of my life,
He is the horizon of my world,
And his love is not a gilded cage.
He holds me, with his open hands,
My soul rests in them freely.

My lover shares my joy with me,
He is the light of my smile,
He is the tickle of my laugh,
And his stories show the world his soul.
He sees me, with his knowing eyes,
I play and dance with him.

My lover shares my tears with me,
He is the holder of my hand,
He is the comfort of my heart,
And his kiss is there to dry each tear.
He feels me, with his tender arms,
My sadness fades into peace,

My lover shares my life with me,
He is the passion of my work,
He is the softness of my rest,
And his life inspires me to live.
He knows me, with his kindred soul,
I never walk my path alone.

Wedding Vows

In a church made of soft earth and open sky,
And God alone as my witness, I make my vows to you.

In this place, with all the world and heaven before us,
Before the God who knows my heart, I open it freely to you.

In the name of everything that is true and right,
Keeping God's faithfulness always, I give my life to you.

In all my sleeping and waking moments,
With my body which God has created, I cherish you.

In each time of providence or poverty we share,
Steadfast in God's strength to overcome, I will carry you.

In the unknown journey of life, in joy or suffering,
Knowing God's ultimate reward for me, I share it with you.

Prayer

Heaven, sweetly bless this man and woman,
The gifts of love, truth, and wonder throughout life.
May they always know this gift, real and complete,
Hold Love's grace with open hands of true devotion.
The arms of a husband are a gleaming temple,
His beloved may take refuge and shelter there,
Let this wife have lips echoing a sacred chant,
Giving solace to her lover in the darkness of night.
Sanctify the morning sun that greets this union,
Blanket with amber glow their holy embrace.
Love from God's own heart, surpassing all others,
Breathe life to this marriage from within
The vows they make to love, honor and cherish.
Mercy from the Lord, enter in times of trial
Bearing comfort and steadfast assurance,
Keep their steps together in Your Perfect Way.
Holy Spirit, sing through their words and deeds
To make their world resound with Joy,
Fruit of their commitment to You and one another.
All-Knowing Trinity, renew their love forever,
Making the end of life only the start of Paradise.
Eternal Fire, burn warm and bright within these souls,
Praising the miracle of their love without question,
You have joined them in Your Perfect Time.

www.ingramcontent.com/pod-product-compliance
Lightning Source LLC
Chambersburg PA
CBHW051938150726
47999CB00006B/2270